a nuclear family

april naoko heck

To Anne:
fellow (IMD) alum + poet: what a joy
to share this day!

Warmly
april naoko heck
April in December
2015

P.O. Box 200340
Brooklyn, NY 11220
www.upsetpress.org

Cover art by Bianca Stone (poetrycomics.com)
Book design by Wendy Lee

UpSet Press is an independent press based in Brooklyn. The original impetus of the press was to upset the status quo through literature. The Press has expanded its mission to promote new work by new authors; the first works, or complete works, of established authors, especially restoring to print new editions of important texts; and first-time translations of works into English. Overall, the Press endeavors to advance authors' innovative visions and works that engender new directions in literature.

Established in 2000, UpSet Press organized readings and writing workshops until 2005 when it published its first book, *Theater of War*, by Nicholas Powers. The Press has increased its publishing efforts in recent years and has multiple titles forthcoming in 2014 and beyond. The University of Arkansas Press became the official distributor of UpSet Press in 2011. For more information, visit upsetpress.org.

Library of Congress Control Number: 2013939709

ISBN 978-1-937357-91-7
Printed in the United States of America

Contents

Acknowledgments

Many thanks to the editors of the following journals for giving a home to my poems.

Artful Dodge: "Notes on the Pacific War"

The Asian American Literary Review: "All day people poured into Asano Park," "Conversation with my Mother," "Distances," "The Innkeeper," "Leaf Book," "Fall Retreat," "Translation," "Winter Recess"

Borderlands: Texas Quarterly Review: "Between Morning Prayers," "The Dragonfly" (as "Libelle")

The Collagist: "Battle at Biak, New Guinea"

The Cream City Review: "Fishermen Lighting Fires on the Lake"

Cura: "Early August, 1945," [Then my mother told me]

Epiphany: "Some Answers," "The Squirrel"

The Greensboro Review: [When she peeled back] (as "The Bridge")

Kartika: "How We Survived the War"

Shenandoah: "The Bells," "The Groundhog"

Whiskey Island: "Sleeping In"

"9/11/11" and "9/12/11" were written for a collaborative group performance, "Together We Are New York," sponsored by Kundiman and made possible in part by funds from the Lower Manhattan Cultural Council.

- - -

[All day people poured into Asano Park] is after John Hersey's *Hiroshima* and Marc Kaminsky's *The Road from Hiroshima*.

"How We Survived the War" is after Julie Otuska's *Buddha in the Attic*.

"I Don't Have Hands That Caress My Face" is after a photograph of the same title by Mario Giacomelli.

- - -

I am grateful for invaluable support from many people, as mentors and muses, fellows and friends: my writing professors at the College of Wooster, University of North Carolina at Greensboro, and University of Maryland; the writers, editors, and artists involved with this book—Elizabeth Arnold, Robert Booras, Natalie Diaz, Rachel Eliza Griffiths, Kimiko Hahn, Wendy Lee, Gerald Maa, Zohra Saed, Bianca Stone, and Chuck Wachtel; my dear friends, including Josephine Bentivegna, Natalie Casale-Altieri, Cathy Linh Che, Leigh Anne Couch, Isabell May, Carly Peterson, and Purvi Shah; the NYU Creative Writing Program community; and Kundiman fellows, affiliates, and faculty. I am especially grateful to my family—my mother Reiko and late father David, and Julie, Yasu, Mattie, and precious Izumi. This book is dedicated to them with love.

Foreword

I've been waiting for this first book for a long time, as a friend, I confess, as well as a fan of the work. Of course the poems should speak for themselves, and they do.

Fabric and flesh bind together the poems in this book. One of this collection's most affecting poems presents a scarf that is washed in a river only to unravel: "one seam came undone, / that is, the entire cloth / dissolved in her hands." Throughout this book, we can see April Naoko Heck's hands likewise, holding something woven for use and for beauty. Her hands hold works woven with threads historical, personal, spirited, and aesthetic. Like the cloth in the nurturing mother's hands, each poem is in a precarious state because its constituent parts are so delicate and interdependent upon each other. A woman brought the soon-to-be-dissolved scarf to the shore having just breastfed her baby in Asano Park, the place to which she fled as haven from the nuclear bomb dropped on Hiroshima. These poems always occur at a moment just beyond or before stability, probably due to April's relentless call to figure loss, especially the singular, yet commonplace, instances of material loss compelled by seemingly immaterial forces, such as history, family, and words. The book's most shocking image is a fabric's pattern seared onto its wearer's skin by an atomic flash. This work hearkens back the more archaic definitions of 'knit' that speak of summing together knowledge and emotions concisely and with purpose.

Coined in the nineteenth century, "nuclear" is a thoroughly modern word. The most prominent valences of this word for this book—

the weapon and the family—are twentieth century concepts. In an essay on poetry and the nuclear age, Allen Grossman defines the nuclear age by its "unalienable capacity for precisely measureless violence" and designates institutions of holiness and structures of poetry as the two cultural forces capable of checking modern warfare's capacity to completely obliterate the image of human beings. For April, "nuclear" is a pharmakon of a word here, designating the most destructive of human inventions and the most restorative of human structures. Her poems attest to Grossman's claim that "poetic culture is a primary custodian of the human image." For April, the humans include her family, war victims, strangers, lovers, loved ones, ones of the imagination, and even versions of her past self. The poems set in World War II Japan effloresce into those set in April's childhood, under paternal eyes, and her adult years. *A Nuclear Family*, then, is a book about and for posterity in the most fundamental way.

If this book displays a thoroughly modern mind, it is one completely indebted to the past. The chronological bookends are World War II and September 12, 2011. Like Benjamin's angel of history, April is poised to move forward in time only able to look back, blown into the future by winds that come from a paradise before her eyes, but out of reach. The penultimate poem speaks of and to a future poem. The poem itself responds with a frank assertion of its own beauty and truth. The surprise here is that the poem can sustain, and then bolster, the sincerity and sentiment without collapsing into sentimental rubble. When the future poem materializes into its present form, the final lines recall the words of Keats' urn without the legendary irony and indeterminacy. What place does that most enigmatic of Grecian urns have for us today? This is a question about poetry and history, about poetic tradition, about the past, present, and future. April asks such questions of herself with such care and persistence, and the poems here reply with melodies, heard and unheard, in due kind.

— Gerald Maa
Irvine, California
March 3, 2013

in the town of six
rivers we melted
pots and pans for gun
metal rationed match
sticks grew hogs and
radishes in school
yards in the desert
town we struck
a steel tower vapor-
ized its stories in
the nowhere town
fistfuls of silver
sewing needles fused
together eyeless

I

Early August, 1945

for Obaasan, my great-grandmother

She lives with her daughter and son-in-law in a two-room house
that has lost one member but will soon gain another—
her girl is pregnant with her first child, my mother.

One night, a knock on the door, a young man with a letter,
another call for volunteers.

Is "volunteers" in quotation marks?

Each household must send one person to Hiroshima
the next morning. Bring rope, the letter says.

Her son-in-law rips the letter in half, refuses to go.
Swears the family's sacrificed enough.

Later, when no one's looking, she pastes the words together
with a smear of soft rice. With her daughter pregnant,

Obaasan elects herself to go.
Who else will obey the emperor's command?

Distances

Like ripples a stone
hitting water makes—
concentric circles on a map.

There's Koi Station, where
Obaasan was ordered off the train
with all of the volunteers

when the drill sounded.
"2.5 kilometers" the map says.
But, "Obaasan was about one *ri* away,"

my mother wrote in a letter
when I told her
what I was writing.

"One *ri* is 3.9 kilometers."
I did the math.
Had the train station moved?

No, the map's dated 1945.
And she walked *toward* the city
carrying rope in her hand.

At 2.5 kilometers,
wood and cloth
scorched black,

the air 50 times hotter
than sunlight
on a summer day.

Ginkaguchi (Temple of the Silver Pavilion)

On beds of moss the gardener minds
with diligence, pink petals sleep.
Brightened by his broom's clean sweep
their falling must appear designed.

But why the temple isn't silver
is strange he thinks—it's still dull wood.
Where the monks first knelt or stood
the sea of sand alone is silver.

With every wind that shimmers ponds,
the lines he rakes and straightens change.
The roof stays plain. He must arrange
the grounds for gods to walk upon.

The Bells

My mother a nugget. Boygirl. Silken bean.
In utero, did she stir?
as her cells divided, tiny buds of limbs:
sprig, branch, vein, opening
and closing, present and tense.

When the bomb struck twenty miles away
and the house's paper doors sailed
in their wood tracks, wheezed shut,
when the other thing divided, subtracted—
did she hear?

Beyond my mother in her mother in the house,
a horse snapped its tail at a blue fly.
The fly spun away, lit the bark of a willow tree.
A leaf dropped, a long leaf stayed.
A narrow canal flowed over stone.

In utero, was she still?
or did she swing in a warm blood sac
as her mother paced the room,
before she would look for her mother in the city,
before white light and black rain were named.

Egg within egg, seed in blind seed,
the child whose name would be
Reiko, meaning the sound of ringing bells.
Now I imagine, as the great wind gusted,
the bronze bell at Otake's shrine

swayed and tolled, and the ringing widened
like waves a stone hitting water starts—out and out—
traveling more slowly than light, singing
as far as the melon field and pasture
where the horses didn't burn.

*

When she peeled back
the sleeves of her blouse,

the pattern of the cloth
according to its dark and light places

was etched into her skin.

*

After years, she would still hold up her hands
and flutter her fingers to describe what she saw,

pale blue light dropped through the sky,
Kira-kira, she said. Twinkle, twinkle.

Conversation with my Mother

How much fabric was left?

    Not much. *Boro-boro*, Obaasan said. Shreds.

And your mother recognized her by the fabric?

    Yes.

If the fabric was in shreds, she was almost naked?

    No, she wore white cotton undergarments.

And they still covered her body?

    They covered her body.

They weren't torn like her blouse and pants?

    They covered her body.

What did the pattern of the fabric look like?

    I don't remember, but it couldn't have been beautiful.

    The emperor wouldn't allow decorative clothing

        during the war.

So the pattern wasn't pretty, not mountain peaks, or sparrows

    on branches?

    She might have used the fabric of a fancy dress to make

        work clothes, like the jacket Higuchi-san made for you.

Was it plain? Was it the fabric's texture, not pattern, that showed

    on her skin?

    No, the fabric was patterned, and the pattern burned into

        her skin.

Maybe flowers?

    Maybe flowers.

Maybe leaves?

    Maybe leaves.

*

All day people poured into Asano Park
drawn to the green coolness and shelter
of leaves. No one, not even children cried,
that is, very few people cried, or talked.

The figure on the ground was a woman.
Her baby unbuttoned her blouse and drank,
that is, her baby clutched at her
bare breast and drank.

When she rinsed her scarf in the river,
one seam came undone,
that is, the entire cloth
dissolved in her hands.

*

Then my mother said:

"When my mother walked to the temple
to search among the people lying in rows,
she barely recognized her mother.

'Is that *you?*' my mother said.
A monk gave them a skull from the crematorium,
prescribed crushed bone for burns.

Just as one neighbor believed in ground potato as a salve
and another ate pounds of tomatoes,
Obaasan believed that the bone saved her.

'It was like lightning,' she'd always say, 'must've been electricity.'"

Perry Nuclear Power Plant

Its plume turns gold as fresh tapped beer
when the sun sets on the plant.
My father worked there seven years,
five more than he had planned.

The cloud shifts shape with wind and light
but always hovers there,
the steam from cooling-tower heights,
their ominous air.

When I was young, I thought that he
worked in the concrete mass.
No in or out that I could see,
no view of sky or grass

until he brought me to his work,
the square that was his room.
I played with pencils at his desk,
drew a cloud, a mushroom.

Again he told how atoms split,
how energy's released.
I yawned and linked his paperclips.
He didn't seem so pleased.

His job was making fission safe,
defuse a ticking bomb.
A stern expression on his face—
I longed instead for mom

who now can see from her backyard
the cloud beyond the trees
which marks the place where he worked hard
and shows a plant at peace.

Fall Retreat

"Use room temperature water," someone says, "never ice."
I must be on fire—"skin holds heat"—
in the mirror my hairline's singed. Lashes, stubs.
Burnt hair smells like eggs I'd meant to fry
on this old gas stove. Sink water won't pour
fast enough, I kneel to turn my face up
under the bathtub's faucet. I'd wanted to visit
the fields, palm sugar to the horses.

—what sent me reeling back, the oven's flash
or pressure, the heat or fear? Obaasan fell forward
but that was a great wind, that was outside;
I'm in a house, I've hurt only myself.
Hard to remember the spark, the tipping,
if the arms flew up or down. A spot on Obaasan's cheek
never healed and wept. I'd wanted to see the fall
leaves, to pick apples in the orchards.

My sleeves are soaked at the wrists, I'm given oxygen.
"The warmth of the skin is normal," the medic says.
"We don't have a mirror." He's lying,
my face is ruined. "Deep breaths."
The truck ceiling is metal, patterned, a kind of braille
I want to touch—what my dad must have seen.
Could he feel his face? Afterward, what if
there were no trucks? Who'd save us
wandering between a canal and sweet potato fields?
They say lilies bloomed in the ashes.

How We Survived the War

we held up our hands, we waved our handkerchiefs like flags, we let our orphans babble and cry on straw mats, we stepped across the flattened neighborhoods, the fragmented, the smashed, we tiptoed over bones of neighbors, umbrella spines, scorched radish gardens, we flashed our scars, we turned our porcelain bellies up like fish, like prey in the *kuma*'s teeth, we prayed, we stayed, we dragged our twisted tricycles behind us, we set up school desks where the school used to be, our babies smiled for the newsman's camera, we didn't believe in the sincerity of red canna flowers blooming too soon, we did not bow, we bowed, we had no sweet *azuki* cakes, no milk candy, we heard wind blow through hulls of streetcars like hollowed carp, we wore long sleeves, we let them fall over our fingertips, we dug in the river sand with our one good hand, we mistrusted the river's mirror surface, we eloped with the enemy, we forgot, we bore babies pink-white as rabbit ears, we strapped them on our backs, our mothers disowned us, we tried new recipes, we tasted applesauce, we let our husbands love us, we waited up when they drank late in corner bars, we stayed home, we learned to drive, we rubbed cocoa butter on stretch marks, we felt safe, we visited national parks, we fed the deer, the tame animals

During the Reconstruction

My grandmother loved the sound of American soldiers singing,
until her daughter married one, that is, ran away. That pink-
white man.

She broke her silence seeing me, her new lopsided granddaughter,
leg in a brace. She called our home a mess and wouldn't help clean it.

A neighbor woman cooked and washed instead, hung laundry
against a blue mountain view. The little *gaijin* cried.

The Leaf Book

In the fall of third grade, when my teacher
assigns the leaf-book project—collect
and name at least a dozen tree leaves—
my dad drives our family to an arboretum,
he brings a field guide and we're all leaf-picking,
all saying *gingko, chestnut, walnut, buckeye.*
Mama writes down American names,
learns too that rootbeer-scented sassafras bear
three kinds of leaves: mittens, gloves, and palms.

The night before my book's due, he stays up.
He helps sort leaf after leaf, irons them
between waxpaper pages he's cut.
Within the circular light of a lamp
he grows younger, I grow older,
typing labels, tracing diagrams.
Does he know that my teacher will show
my book to the class? that I'm looked at
enough, the one mixed kid? They'll stare

like they stared when I was called from class
to be tested for the "gifted program."
I rose from my chair, carrying the too-big,
man's leather briefcase he'd loaned to me
for good luck. But like the kids' snickers
it only confused me. The test did too:
"Can you name three things made of aluminum?" "No."
"How tall is the average man?" I answered
with all I knew, my own height, "Four feet tall."

When I told my dad I'd failed, he called
my principal: "Your test is wrong," he said,
"This is your regional spelling champ,
honor roll student, first chair in band."
He listed bell choir, softball, swim team,
even states and countries I'd seen. But I have to try
harder, I know the wrong kinds of love:
scarlet oak, white oak, black oak, laurel and pin,
memorized by size and color, lobe and vein.

I Don't Have Hands That Caress My Face

Today, on winter's first snowfall,
it's no coincidence
that the young seminarians
in bell-shaped robes
appear as heavy as
the trees behind them,
brother and trunk falling
black against the sharp white yard.
Think of the darkness of a life without
hands that caress your face,
arms like branches
reaching without touch;
think of sleep, the body
inside the hollow body of nights.
Only snow will kiss this
figure in the center
of the camera's eye, the boy
with arms flung open
to embrace air—
and because his face
is loveliest, because like Adam
he offers a rib to make a space
for God, you want to be like that, that good.

Mushroom Cloud

When Mount St. Helens thunders and snows gray ash over
    the picnic table
When I scrape a handful into a glass jar as a souvenir
When the stores sell out of brooms and shovels
When a lava-river bulldozes houses and its coal-crust glows
When the dome goes quiet again
When it wakes up again and hoof-prints track the page of a hill
When a photographer crouches in the nose of a small plane
When a doe folds like a note
When a paper deer
When the soft whites of
When fallen at the height of
When we're moving away again and I don't know why
When all summer the wild, wide blue of lakes fill with mud
    and woods

Winter Recess

Jimmy Carter's in office
meaning my dad's still job hunting,
meaning I get him to myself these days.
He takes me to see Lake Erie frozen,
the heaped shore the waves have sculpted,
white tundra and half-circle of horizon beyond, immense—
the stillness is dense, church-hushed.
We hike, kicking ice clumps that break open,
showing rows of tiny pale-green glass pipes.
One frozen crest splashes water,
glossing layer on layer, making itself.
It's safe, he says, though I wonder
at the rest of the lake beneath our feet,
where grease ice and slush
must heave like labored breath,
with the weight of centuries
of changing shapes and names:
Lake Maumee, Arkona, Whittsley, Wayne.
I've learned them in school,
how Erie won't last long in geological time,
the clay cliffs where swallows nest are dissolving.
Months before the electric company
hires him, I think he hopes I'll know
more forms of water than worry.
Tomorrow, he says, *we'll bring your sled.*

That New Year's Eve

My dad buckled the good car into a telephone pole.
Drunk. Alone. Did he mean to teach me?
The roads were snow-drifted, black ice
hidden. With their siren flashing, silenced,
two cops dropped him home. Mama said his name
with a question mark when he walked in.
He punched a door, the hollow plywood caved.
A hole that we cover with a Christmas wreath year round.

Breakfast

My dad throws
a box of cereal.
It just misses

my head.
The shoehorn
flies by.

Another touch-and-go day
when a hangover
clouds his aim,

Valium slows
his arm.
Chew, I think to myself,

Drink your tea.
It's only
the weather,

morning hail or calm.

Dear Self

I wish I had found you
there in the snowfall

crossing the white field
to your dormitory hall

I'm sitting on the edge
of your hard twin bed

I'm packing your suitcase
I'm leaving out the black dress

When somebody called
the school switchboard

your dad   *an aneurysm*   *go home*

*

On the day he wakes,
the nurse props him in a chair.
He sips apple juice

as she holds the little cup.
And though his head lists
and his eyes won't focus,

for a moment
there's a look, recognition.
We're giddy, we're quick.

Love you too he says.

*

After the surgery
he'd improved at first
but now he's worse.

We eat in the cafeteria.
We ride the elevator
up to his floor.

The doctor says, *It's time.*
One more hour maybe
or, with his strong heart,

it's gone this long, two.

Funeral Outfit

Did I try on the white blouse, did I pay
with cash, did I drive to the store, did my little
sister come, did I tell the cashier
what it was for, did I
wear it again, did it stain, did it match,
did I wash it first, did it fit, was it
pretty, was it from the girls' department or women's,
were the buttons milk or pearls, did I think
anyone ever would kiss me, did I look at my father's
face, did I cue the song, had he warned me,
did it match his silk pillow, did it itch,
was it lace, was it proper, did I sit
next to his mother, was there coffee after, were there lilies,
were there windows overlooking a parking lot,
grass mowed down by the neighbor boy?

The Beaver

What I remember most
is the skin, not just bloodless
and gray, more grayish tinged
yellow from somewhere far

beneath, like the skin I've seen
lately of the animal floating
belly-up in a nearby creek.
A beaver, I think, but the face

is hidden, head tilted back
too far to be sure. A hill
of torso pokes through the surface,
mashed fur and nipple,

perfect ridges of rib
like a tiny man's. It wants me
to look away, it won't go away,
the cold, still water scummed

with night's ice preserves it,
my mummy, my memory
waiting for me to pause
on the creek's mud bank.

Smoke

The sweet spice of Marlboro Reds,
the carton under his driver's seat:
as a kid I loved to tug a new pack's
gold ribbon, the crisp of cellophane wrap.
How the lid flipped open, the foil peeled and snapped.
I learned to turn the box upside-down,
smack it on my palm, tap the tobacco tight.
With one hand light a match in its book,
pinch my cigarette between finger and thumb:
each gesture, each drag would pull him back.

Spring Break at the Ponce de Leon Motel

—Tallahassee, Florida

The "Triple-A-Approved" sign
is rusted, toppled
into weeds. The pool gate
is left open late.
We sit by the water
as if it's the ocean,
I'm an orphan
telling its surface
how lack defines
me, a hole
in my side.
The moss-draped trees,
the purple beards of wisteria
make me confess,
point to my rib—
on the motel roof
Ponce de Leon points too,
his conquistador hat
faded to pastels.
It's snowing up north
where we've come from.
You listen, that is
you hear me
say words that mean
other words: *I want to rise
into that twilight* means *drown.*

The Dragonfly

Libelle: German for dragonfly.
Liberate me. Ring the bell of the air
with your wings. Fair southern belle, whirl
your gossamer skirt by the lily pond.

Elle: French for she.
She, dragonfly, daughter of sky and water,
marries her reflection, her loneliness.
No one can catch her.

Li: first name of a Chinese poet.
Li says the dragonfly
is the place in the air
where air longs to be.

Lie: English for false, a veil.
I tuck the past under my wing,
now I'm too heavy to fly.
Lapis-blue shiver,

little aircraft, transport me,
carry me on your back
to the high summer clouds, sailing
somewhere between this life and after.

Fishermen Lighting Fires on the Lake

There is no plot, there are no characters,
just a man at a table trying to write,
his whiskey paling around cubes of ice,
turning the color of fields in fall.
Just a woman in the next room
reading news she'll forget before closing

her eyes to sleep. No extraordinary
joy here, only June pouring bright
against the windowpanes,
voices roaming the street below,
city sounds that remind the man of first love,
the woman of her father looking down

from heaven. Maybe you want angels
and nirvana, you want a madman
poking scissors into a Picasso in daylight,
pieces of canvas like a broken sky.
You want the woman to harbor a secret
in her heart, she's in love with two men,

she's Anna in a city with no trains,
there are buses and yellow taxis,
children on bicycles that make her wistful,
why can't it be summertime all year, always
the trees blooming green?
You want to know what the man writes,

how he struggles over the phrase
"fishermen lighting fires on the lake."
He means a frozen lake, but that's too much,
he means the sputter of light on snow,
the patience of men, the airy grace
of nature. There's no mystery, no sickness,

no epiphany here: after midnight
the man might retire his pen, rub his eyes.
He might drink a glass of water before
quietly pulling the cool sheet back
from her body, climbing into bed
beside her as he has every night

for seven years, which might be a long time
to love a person, a lake might be the closest
thing to describe the feeling
in his chest, clutching at the moment
that is almost over
as he touches his lips to her forehead.

He knows she's tired, she doesn't stir
to open her arms; he lets her sleep, envious
of her slow breathing as he rests
his body in a straight line, trying not to think
of everything at once, how "frozen"
will not do, all the hours behind him,

water swallowing the skyline
along the shore of his city.
How teachers told him in school
"if you go not to Jerusalem
Jerusalem is still there," the far-off
golden places swimming behind his eyes.

Sleeping In

High windows,
glass white with morning sun.

Church bells ring over the city,
the day half gone.

Who walked below
on the shoulders of streets,

who woke early
to see a rose-washed sky?

Where are they now?
Beyond the train yard,

beyond the school
abandoned for summer.

There are moments when
to lie beside someone

is to sleep curled inside a leaf.

The Innkeeper

My last morning in London, over breakfast,
the innkeeper's telling me more about his late daughter.
At our first breakfast, he and his wife
had threaded her name through our talk,
their hands and bodies still for politeness,
a word's weight, "cancer," making them still.
Absence welled like the atmosphere of the house-
turned-guesthouse, a dampness or chill,
vague scent of cedar tucked in a drawer.
Had they read knowledge of loss on my face,
felt invited to confide? Or did they talk of her
to every guest, diminish grief by repetition?
She would've been my age—my late father, his.

I remember how I'd arrived late at night,
exhausted, my suitcase lost. He knew my name,
gave directions to town, showed my room
where tea and blankets warmed spirit and bone.
The next day, he and his wife drove me
to Hampstead Heath. She rested on a bench
by the lake, preferring, like my mother,
a view of ducks and geese. He and I walked,
among hedgerows and swimming ponds,
tree and tree-root gnarled into animal shapes,
like forms half-seen in clouds. "These woods and trails,"
he said "untouched for years—" He looked pleased
as if he'd made them, pleased by my listening.

At the breakfast table now, drinking what's left
of my coffee, I say, "On Christmas morning
I dreamed so clearly my dad had died
I woke up. I went to my parents' room.
The covers were warm, but I tapped him
awake to be sure. Two weeks later—
it was quick. They really tried."
I look at him, the antique windows behind him
blooming with gray, early spring light,
as if rain, at any moment, might lash
and bead the thick warped pane, as if
something less than glass separated us
from the lost father and daughter
who regarded us now—I was certain—
regarding each other.

Hair

In the first poem I made a kite with it,
flew it into the sky.

In the second poem it talked,
I told it to shut up.

In the third poem it talked again!
and I listened to it—my father's blond hair

in a baggie on my closet shelf—
it wanted to know why

a nurse gave it to me
with his clothes, a black comb.

Not Robert-Redford hair,
not prom- or catch-you-later-hair

but heavy, a little meaty
to the touch.

Maybe I should stuff a voodoo doll with it,
or give it to birds

to coil in their nests.
Or what if I threw it like ashes into water?

Ate it like bread
and got fat?

Think I'll put it on my head, do a rock-step,
one-two,

forgive us both
for this long separation—

Thread

"A scientist in the true sense needs to be in love with a rich store of data." —Wallace Chafe

It won't love you back,
not Chapel Hill, a hill, old dive
or bartender whose turntable changed
your life. Not fields of silver
queen corn raked
by wind, a certain moon
or moonlessness, a bend
in the road, left turn, fork,
kiss. Many kisses. A kitchen,
lemon wedges and salt.
The small dog that darted
into the road. A folded body,
the roommate who carried it
away. Closets full of data,
dates, datelessness shoved
in a shoebox, spare shelf,
life-swell, a knot
catches in the throat.
What's lost, reinvented:
windspill, cloudburst, thread-of-milk.
How I knew my way
to a grave I'd never seen.

IV

Notes on the Pacific War

Hirohito is a giant yellow-bellied bean hung on a line.

Hirohito is a bucktooth rat with *Nip* branded on his side.

Hirohito is suicide.

Hirohito is volunteer nurses who hide in caves and refuse to
wave handkerchiefs.

Hirohito is not Magic Diplomatic Summary.

Hirohito is not Intercept.

Hirohito is not Project.

Hirohito is not Stalin saying *finis Japs*.

Hirohito is not Truman saying *A rain of ruin from the air as the
world has never seen.*

Hirohito is a rain of ruin from the air as the world has never seen.

Hirohito, 10,000 Americans injured or dead.

Hirohito, typhoon winds that blew back Genghis Khan are now
two-thousand kamikazes cartwheeling down to ships.

Hirohito, the curved jewel.

Hirohito, the circular mirror.

Hirohito is three strongholds, no nine, no thirteen on a
southern island.

Hirohito can barely see from his little eyes!

Hirohito is a hairy black spider with radioactive feet!

Hirohito say *sayonara*, say bye-bye.

When Hirohito makes a radio address he says *Well things didn't go
as planned* and children hear the voice of the sun for the
first time.

Hirohito is a country carrying a country on her back like a sack
of burnt yams.

Of the Emperor Hirohito, Obaasan always said *Don't look into
God's eyes, you will go blind.*

Yam

Blind mole, her potato body
shaped like my body,
calls me callous.

I am what I am, mama
of whiskery root,
small-eyed, pucker-mouthed.

But a little heat will
soften the meat.
I am a golden yam.

My pale sister, *yamaimo*.
From mountains she's taken raw,
snowfall in a blue clay bowl.

But elsewhere, of flat fields that men sow,
I am the pain under a rib
if eaten raw, the acidic bite

of fresh flesh.

Battle at Biak, New Guinea

In the strategic shelter of hillside caves
my great-grandfather's infantry starves.
The 2-2-2. On this island of coral reef.
In heatstroke jungle, in mangrove swamps.
Rumors of Japanese ships—but no ships.
Birds of paradise thrive.
Sun thrives. Ulcers thrive. His dogs' ribs
are sharp as blades. These animals
won't be saved. This island. This airfield.
This ghost of a shore. Rumors of reinforcements,
no reinforcements. Dogs guide snipers at night.
But no ships, no ships, Colonel, the men
are starved. Gasoline trickling into tunnels,
matches thrown at caves' mouths.
The flag must burn. The grave, dug.
It was a pistol he used, no, a knife.
It was a bundle of letters he sent. It was the sun.
Somebody, a soldier, told what he saw,
saw what needed to be told.
Harikiri. A knife, no, a pistol.
His wife held his hat. My mother held a flag.
They remembered the house in Manchuria.
Servants. Running water. Remembered the sun,
no, a spoonful of dirt. He fell, somewhere
he fell, fattened the jungle with his pride.

*

where is the body

                            no record of the body

where is the body

                            the body is the record

what is the body

                            the emperor's hand

what is the body

                            the body is the question

Some Answers

I don't remember, I was in a blackout.

I don't remember, the city was in a blackout.

I don't like myself very much.

I don't like your wife very much.

We climbed down forty-three flights of stairs.

We walked five miles in paper-thin sandals.

This way to the train station.

This way to the park where trees will hide us from planes.

True, the signs are confusing in that part of town.

There were x's marked on the eyelids, that's how I knew the
      people were dead.

Because I prefer whiskey to gin.

Because the horse wasn't close to the fire.

Because her ten fingers flamed blue toward heaven.

Because pomegranates, when ripe, split open easily.

Because he was an ordinary white guy.

Because they didn't have any other medicine they used
      mercurochrome.

That's right, they used vegetable oil.

That's right, he took the last rice ball.

He turned the key.

He didn't mean to.

The tomatoes didn't help at all.

Because silk was rare.

Because the priest liked a drink.

Because the hospital was gone.

Like the clouds of ten storms gathering on the horizon.

I only thought I was in love.

The scar on her cheek, reddish-purple, continued to weep.

He told a different version of the story.

The sound of airplanes scares her now.

You should be tender.

You should probably leave.

Look closer.

She has difficulty expressing her feelings.

It never belonged to him anyway.

The Groundhog

—how some names are stories,
how, if you've never seen a groundhog,
you can know *ground* and *hog*,
then find what's missing

in the hairy animal sitting upright,
sniffing air in a neighbor's yard.
A Norwegian friend once told me,
in her language, the word for *goatee*

translates to *porn donut.* I wonder
whatever happened to her
or to that East Village bar?
She dated a boy without a goatee,

without, for that matter, a donut.
A bare branch scrapes the window,
winter's coming and I'm thinking
how my own name means

fourth month and *naive child* and *hell.*
Born in August, what kind of story's that?
My father's name was David
for *beloved*—beloved, hell, his story

is right. Every morning, I'm looking
for the groundhog, for the piggish,
brown ripple across a yard, the dash
under the porch into the dark.

Translation

Some things we know: distances between cities, between Otake
       and Koi,
Koi and Hiroshima, names of stations, the kanji for *atom* reads *child*.

A body lying in the middle of the road, the road,
a scarf, names of lilies, *golden-rayed, stargazer, demon girl, baby deer.*

We know drawings, bicycles, animals on fire, a woman calling
across a rubble field, *Husband forgive me for leaving,*

puppets, buttons, blind fish walking in the hills, shoes—
always shoes—umbrella menders, a boy holds a bucket of sand.

Abi kyo kan no chimata Obaasan always said about that day.
There are some things I don't know, so my mother tells me,

"*No chimata* means *all around myself. Kyo* means *cry. Kan* means *cry.*
Abi means *avici*, the eighth and lowest Buddhist hell of hells."

Where there's no light of the lighthouse that shines on the cape,
no light of a pyre, silk, mother's eye, or freshly rinsed gauze,

but the gleam of an iron fortress, an iron rack, a place of iron
       birds and foxes,
where the fire dog races east to west. No time and no space,

it's un-spaced and ceaseless: flaming serpents wrapped around
    a neck,
sword mountains and sword trees, thorn and razor streams,
    molten iron to drink.

Prayer to the God of Mochi

If stars are rice grains in the night sky,

      and spaces between them a blue alphabet of fish broths,

if constellations are hymnals and hymnals are open to the right song,

if there is an opposite for *choke*,

if throat is a kind of bird, a swallow,

if sweet is synonym for salt, and salt

      for paddies underwater reflecting Kochi's planting-season sky,

if a saucer is a story, and a fork its tragic ending,

if the hero dies and leaves the women to run straw-households full

      of children and piano lessons,

if pan-fried in a black jacket of seaweed, if burnt

      on the bilingual tongue,

if I'm homesick times two,

-

if the milk of my white man is my favorite dessert,

-

if mochi cakes are miniature white mattresses,

if heat softens them to feather and fluff,

if beds could really fly,

if each grain has two eyes and a mouth,

if they circle the land like spirits of the ocean's lost,

if mochi is glue and fate is the glue that binds us,

-

if no elderly will choke on tradition this new year,

if, dear gods, you will protect them, sweep the heavy snow

      from their steps and roofs,

-

if my mother is wrong and I am, in fact, good, safe,

then let your fountains drink my yen and dollar coins,
then read the wishes I have penned on your wooden tablets,
then hear my thank yous in the tongues I know,
then make my words neither bitter nor too sweet,
then lend me your mortar and pestle,

    let me fill the small porcelain plates,

then teach me about flour and daily sustenance,
then fill the festival's hanging baskets with glowing coals,

    light the night and cherry tree, bless the cooks

    turning skewers over bluegold flames.

The Squirrel

There's a dead, or dying squirrel in a tree
eye-level with my bedroom window.
Its tail moves when the wind moves. Three days now,
I wonder if it breathes or deflates, a husk of fur.
I want the leaves again at my window, I want
to not want a thing. A starlet says she looks forward
to her thirties, she lies. Who wouldn't give up
knowing for time? When I was younger
I jumped into love like a summer lake,
I wouldn't do it again. I would do it again.
I dove into a water-flooded quarry,
I climbed its limestone cliffs. People said
a truck lay rusting at the bottom, who drove it in?
The summer I worked on Mackinac Island,
I rode my flat-tired bike downhill and pushed it up.
Why bother, I thought, it worked half the time
until someone sailed it off the end of a dock.
Only locals stayed through winter,
sledding the path of old Christmas trees
across the frozen lake.
I'd have cheated on my boyfriend
but no one would have me
on that all-white island. I mean,
it was as if I saw the path of pines
lie down, pointing the way inland.
Once I walked into the house next door
where four college boys lived.

I sat on their sofa and stared at the TV.
I wanted something no one can give.
What did they know about sickness,
the ache held tight in my throat?
An eight-mile path circled the island,
I ran and ran, the sun dropped and turned
the water to milk, the end was the beginning.

9 / 11 / 11

Upon being asked to write a 9/11 poem, I consulted a recent
National Book Award winner.

I stood on the wide beach and asked the ocean for its best advice.

I'm not up to this task, I told my future-poem. What can I
possibly say?

But you've written about war before, someone said—I think it was
me or the poem—

Your great-grandmother, a survivor. Your great-grandfather, lost in
the Pacific War.

I tried to outrun the hurricane, I shored up my doors.

How about writing about fathers instead, said my poem, a hard-
working father, say, driving a taxi every day?

I don't want to be sad, I said, my father passed away, every father
reminds me of him.

I hate you, poem, for wanting to know the truth.

The truth is, I trusted the sky.

Trusted it wouldn't throw things at us, a bitter god hurling stones.

Remember that story, I said to no one, "The Lottery" by
  Shirley Jackson?

The townspeople kill one of their own.

And remember the Canada geese incident? I said again to no one.

Some officials thought geese caused the plane crash in the Hudson.

Some officials gassed all the geese.

One day the lake was quiet.

What is wrong with you, I said, confusing my pronouns.

We're talking about people, not geese, not gas, not, geez, where
  were we?

gas chambers—flight—falling—

And the poem said, how will you make sense of geese and fathers
  and planes?

Why not, while you're at it, mention how boys called you chink
  on the playground?

Poem, you are a fucking mess, I said.

Oh no, I'm beautiful, it said, I'm the truest thing you've said for days.

9/12/11

What I meant by the hundreds of Canada geese disappearing is: intuition.

An obsession. I couldn't let it go.

Extermination as metaphor—but for what? for whom?

The lake was quiet one day.

I'd hardly realized my love for the gaggle of voices, the brown bodies cluttering blue, until they were gone.

They're rats with wings, the geese-haters said, did you forget about the crash?

I wrote a letter to the paper.

Why would you gas them all, I said, you with my taxes, my vote.

Take them upstate, I said, take them to—Canada.

They're migratory, they'll come back, the haters said, stop with your bread crumbs, your sentiment.

I know a monk, a groundskeeper of a school.

He's a keeper and killer of geese who pack his ponds and soccer fields.

Every springtime he shakes their eggs—the scrambled, miniature
suns will never hatch.

A metaphor for what? a question of souls?

Or how I can't feel the shell-sharp glass?

I can't feel the sting and ash?

I'm a birdwatcher, and hardly skilled at that.

No binoculars, no field guide.

I like to take walks.

I like to look at the lake and leaves and birds, nature's subtractions
and additions.

If you knew someone in that plane, people said, you would not
be so foolish.

You with your simple heart.

You with your little dog.

Open your eyes.

April Naoko Heck was born in Tokyo and relocated with her family to the U.S. when she was seven. She is a Kundiman Fellow and has been awarded residencies at the Virginia Center for the Creative Arts and Vermont Studio Center. She lives in Brooklyn.